Butterscotch The Sweet Hell

Manon Thomas

PREFACE OF THE PUBLISHER

We are pleased that you have chosen this book. If you are in possession of a paperback book, we will gladly send you the same as an e-book, then you can easily turn the pages digitally as well as normally.

We attach great importance to the fact that all of our authors, when creating their own cookbooks, have recooked all of their recipes several times.
Therefore, the quality of the design of the recipes and the instructions for recooking are detailed and will certainly succeed.

Our authors strive to optimize your recipes, but tastes are and will always be different!

We at Mindful Publishing support the creation of the books, so that the creative authors of the recipes can take their time and enjoy cooking.

We appreciate your opinion about our recipes, so we would appreciate your review of the book and your experience with these great recipes!

In order to reduce the printing costs of our books and to offer the possibility to offer recipes in books at all, we have to do without pictures in the cookbooks. The digital version has the same content as the paperback.

Our recipes will convince you and reveal to you

a culinary style you can't get enough of!

Enough of the foreword, let the recipes begin!

NAKED CAKE CHOCOLATE-CARAMEL

Average level

Ingredients

190g of sugar
1 sachet of vanilla sugar
4 eggs
3 teaspoons of cocoa powder
80g of cornstarch
1 teaspoon baking powder
50cl of liquid cream
4 pinches of salt
2 sheets of gelatin
25g of butter
40g of powdered sugar
100g of mascarpone

Preparation

Separate the whites from the yolks. Mix the yolks with 100 g of sugar and vanilla sugar until the mixture whitens. Add the cornflour and yeast and then the cocoa powder. Beat the egg whites until stiff and fold gently into the dough. Pour into a round mould and bake for 25 to 30 minutes in an oven at 150°C (gas mark 5).

Gently melt 90 g of sugar in the pan, without mixing. When the sugar is completely melted and brown, stop cooking and deglaze with a drizzle of liquid cream.
Add salt, butter and gelatine previously softened.
Whip 25 cl of cream into whipped cream.
Stir in the whipped cream.
Cut the sponge cake into 2 equal discs.
Garnish the first sponge cake with a generous layer of mousse and close with the second sponge cake.
Keep the cake in a cool place for at least one night.
A few hours before serving, whip up 20 cl of cream. Incorporate in turn the powdered sugar then the mascarpone while continuing to whip.
Cover the cake with whipped cream and spread it with a spatula.
Decorate as you like!

CARAMEL MIRABELLES

very easy

Ingredients

1 jar of mirabelle plums
100g of sugar
1 glass of Mirabelle plum brandy liqueur
1 pinch of cinnamon

Preparation

Make a caramel with the juice of mirabelle plums and sugar. When the latter blonded, throw the mirabelle plums in it and let them coat with sugar, sprinkle with cinnamon. Flambé with the mirabelle plum brandy slightly warmed. Put 2 scoops of vanilla ice cream in bowls and pour the mirabelle plums on top. Serve immediately.

VANILLA-CARAMEL AND PINEAPPLE CAKE

easy

Ingredients

1 box of diced pineapples
2 vanilleet caramel
2 jars of yoghurt flour
2 jars of sugar yogurt
1 jar of yoghurt and oil
1 sachet of vanilla sugar
1 sachet of yeast
3 eggs

Preparation

Preheat the oven to 180°C (thermostat 6).
Drain the pineapple, cut into pieces.
Mix the 2 blanks with the sugars, add the whole eggs, flour and baking powder as well as the oil.
Make the preparation homogeneous and add the pineapples.
Butter a large mould and pour the preparation into it. Bake in the oven for 30 minutes (check with the tip of the knife).

EASY CARAMEL MOUSSE

very easy

Ingredients

1 can of sweetened condensed milk
2 eggs

Preparation

Cook the condensed milk in a bain-marie for three hours (it's long but it's worth waiting).
Let it cool a little and add the yolks and then the egg whites which have been stiffened.
Pour into ramekins and leave to set in the refrigerator.

BROWNIES WITH M&M AND CARAMEL COULIS

easy

Ingredients

1 box of sweetened condensed milk 400ml
115g of butter
340g of dark chocolate pastry (50-60%)
450g of sugar
10ml vanilla extract
4 eggs
225g of flour
225g of peanut M&M's

Preparation

Preheat the oven beam to 200°c. Pour the sweetened condensed milk into a baking dish and cover it with aluminium foil. Put it in the oven for 1 hour in a bain-marie, checking the water level often.
Put the butter and chocolate cut into pieces in a microwaveable dish and heat for 2 minutes. The mixture must not boil. Stir gently to remove lumps, then pour the mixture into a salad bowl. Leave to cool a little. Add the sugar and vanilla. Mix Add the eggs. Mix. Pour the flour little by little.
Mix it all together.
Add the M&M's.
Pour the preparation in a going dish and distribute uniformly. Bake in the oven at 180°c for 25min.

LIQUID CARAMEL (CAN BE KEPT WITHOUT HARDENING)

very easy

Ingredients

1 tablespoon of vinegar
500g powdered sugar
12.5cl of water

Preparation

Put the vinegar + sugar + 12.5 cl of water in 1 saucepan.
Heat over high heat for about 15 minutes.
When the caramel turns pale, lower the heat a little and add very, very gently 25 cl of cold water (watch out for splashes).
Heat again for 1 minute over high heat.

APPLE AND CARAMEL SEMOLINA CAKE

very easy

Ingredients

1kg of apple
80g of semi-salted butter
75cl of milk
100g of fine or medium wheat semolina
200g of sugar cubes
100g powdered sugar
1 sachet of vanilla sugar

Preparation

Use a large buttered casserole dish.
Peel and arrange the apples cut into pieces at the bottom of the dish so that they completely cover the bottom. Prepare the caramel (preferably in a frying pan) with the 200 g of sugar cubes and 8 to 10 cl of water. When the caramel is well browned, put the 40 g of semi-salted butter in it at once. Pour this caramel on the apples.
Turn on the oven at 210°C (thermostat 7).
Bring the milk to the boil then add the semolina and bring back to a low heat. Stir until thickening then add the caster sugar, the vanilla sugar and the 40 g of remaining butter.
Pour this mixture in an even layer over the apples and the caramel and put in the oven.
Watch the cooking, it is ready when the semolina

is lightly browned.

APPLE AND CARAMEL SOUP WITH SALTED BUTTER

very easy

Ingredients

1kg of pommeboskoop
50g of buttered butter
120g of sugar
70g of fresh cream
15cl of water

Preparation

Peel the apples, remove the core and cut them into pieces.
Cook them for 15 minutes over medium heat in a covered
saucepan, covering one third of them with water.
In another saucepan, melt the sugar with the 15 cl of
water and let it boil until it takes a golden color.
Reduce the heat, add the salted butter and mix, then
add the fresh cream and mix again until smooth.
Mix the apples with the cooking water
and then stir in the caramel.
It is ready!

SMALL JARS OF CARAMEL CREAM

very easy

Ingredients

1 l of milk
180g of sugar
10 eggs
1 tablespoon of vanilla extract

Preparation

Caramelize a mold with sugar.
Heat 1 liter of milk with 180 g of sugar.
Beat 10 eggs in omelette (calibre 60-65).
Add the eggs and the vanilla to the milk, at about 80°.
Pour the whole while passing it in the caramelized mould.
Cook in a bain-marie at th 4-5 (150°C).
Put in jars.

CLASSIC CARAMEL CREAM

very easy

Ingredients

1 l of milk
1 vanilla bean
6 eggs
14 tablespoons of sugar + 20 pieces

Preparation

Cut the vanilla bean and put it in the milk.
Bring the milk to the boil.
Meanwhile, in a large salad bowl, whip the whole
eggs with the sugar, then add the milk, taking care
not to cook the eggs; remove the vanilla pod.
In a thick-bottomed saucepan, caramelize the sugar cubes
with water, when the caramel is done, line a mould with it.
To pour the apparatus in the caramelized mould and to enfoyer
in the water bath at 180°C for 45 mn approximately.
Ideally the top should remain shiny (mirror) and not colored.
Leave to cool and store in the refrigerator.
Enjoy very fresh.

PERUVIAN CHOCOLATE-CARAMEL AND COFFEE CREAMER

easy

Ingredients

1 l of milk
4 egg yolks
100g caster sugar
1/2 vanilla bean
120g of dessert chocolate
50g of coffee
100g of sugar

Preparation

Bring the milk to the boil with the vanilla. In the meantime, put the coffee beans on low heat in a large saucepan, then pour the boiling vanilla milk over them. Leave to brew for 15 minutes.
In another saucepan, prepare a caramel:
Melt the pieces of sour until the sugar turns brown, then wet the whole with a 10 cl glass of water and simmer while stirring until thickened.
Off the heat, incorporate the chocolate cut

into pieces so that it melts.
Filter the milk and remove the coffee beans.
Add the caramel chocolate.
In a salad bowl, beat the egg yolks with the sugar until it whitens, then pour in the chocolate-caramel milk.
Put everything back in a saucepan and let it thicken over very low heat without boiling.
Let cool then place the cream in the refrigerator.
To taste quite fresh.

EGGS WITH ORANGE PEEL MILK ON A BED OF CARAMEL SPRINKLED WITH THE SCENT OF THE ISLANDS

very easy

Ingredients

1 l of milk
6 eggs
125 g of sugar
1 orange
10 cl of rum
1 sachet of vanilla sugar
Caramel

Preparation

In a first ramekin break your 6 eggs and beat them into an omelette; then grate your orange peel and add it; let it wait. In a first saucepan make your caramel, with your own proportions, 3/4 water, 1/4 sugar; then pour it in your ramekins, put them in the fridge 5 min to harden the caramel.

In a second saucepan, pour your cold milk, mix the sugar and make it boil; when hot, pour the vanilla sugar and the rum. Pour your eggs into the boiling milk while stirring, remove it from the heat, take out your ramekins and fill them. Put them in the oven at thermostat 5 (150°C) for 20 minutes and then at thermostat 1 for 10 minutes, be careful to watch your cooking.
Serve the next day so that the ramekins are full of flavour, with a small sparkling Savoy wine and the famous Nantes butter cookies.
Enjoy your meal!

CARAMEL CREAM WITH ZEB

easy

Ingredients

1 l of milk
6 eggs trails
2 vanilla beans
75 g powdered sugar
1 can of sweetened condensed milk 130 g

Preparation

Heat the milk over low heat with the split vanilla pods, (which makes its small black grains appear, nice aesthetically, but also for the taste), and the sugar, avoid cooking too quickly.
Out of the fire beat the eggs, once well mixed,
add the condensed milk and mix again. Last step,
add the hot milk and remove the pods!
Cook at least one hour at less than 100°C otherwise everything will start to boil (80°C is ideal to avoid boiling).
NB: It must be cooked in an earthenware dish, once the milk has been heated in the pan with the rest (like a paté terrine) that you can see at the butcher's. It should be cooked in a bain-marie, in theory, but the dish alone in the oven is enough, as long as the temperature is respected.

CARAMEL CUSTARD

easy

Ingredients

1l of milk
8 eggs
30 pieces of sugar
1 pinch of salt
1 vanilla bean
10cl of caramel

Preparation

Allow a cooling time (can be done the day before too).
To be made in a 16 cm diameter charlotte mould.
Boil the milk with the vanilla bean split in 2 and the salt.
Remove from the heat. Add the sugar. Leave to infuse.
Eventually make the caramel. You can take some prepared at all, or make it (see recipe after).
Whisk the eggs. Add them to the milk. Stir them together.
Strain through a sieve into the charlotte mould.
Put it in a dish containing water (= bain marie) and cook in a soft oven (thermostat 4) for 1 hour. Neither the water nor the cream should boil. The cooking is ready when a knife blade inserted in the middle comes out clean.
Leave to cool in the mould. Just before serving, run a knife blade around the edges of the pan. Turn onto a serving dish.
Homemade caramel :
Place 18 sugar cubes in a saucepan and moisten with water. Heat gently. Let boil, then thicken. Allow to

become blond, but be careful, as it darkens quickly. When the color is nice, plunge the bottom into a pot of cold water quickly. Stir the mould to line it and cool it in cold water. The caramal must crack everywhere.

CARAMEL RICE CAKE WITH SALTED BUTTERSCOTCH

easy

Ingredients

1l whole milk
200g of sugar
200g round rice dessert or risotto type
1 split vanilla bean or 2 teaspoons of vanilla extract
1 pinch of salt
3 egg trails

Preparation

Make the rice pudding: in a saucepan heat the milk + the 200 g of sugar + the split vanilla bean + the pinch of salt. When it boils, add the rice, lower the heat, and let it cook for 30 minutes on a low heat while stirring from time to time. Leave to cool.
Preheat the oven to 140°C (thermostat 4-5).
Prepare the caramel: in a small saucepan, heat the 100g of sugar and 2 tablespoons of water over high heat. When the caramel has taken a nice dark amber color, remove from the heat, add the 25 g of salted butter while stirring to stop the cooking. Quickly distribute the caramel on the bottom of a 26 cm mould to be missed.
During this time, the rice pudding has cooled enough to be able to incorporate the 3 eggs previously beaten. Pour

the preparation into the mould and cook for 1 hour at 140°C (thermostat 4-5). Take out of the oven, and unmould hot in the serving dish before the caramel freezes.

CARAMEL CREAM

very easy

Ingredients

1l whole milk
7 egg yolks + 2 whole eggs
1 small can of sweetened condensed milk (450 g)
1 vanilla stick
1 sachet of vanilla sugar
Caramel (ready to use)

Preparation

Heat the milk with the vanilla stick and the vanilla sugar (so as to give the milk a nice flavor). Leave to cool.
In a salad bowl, break the 2 whole eggs + the 7 egg yolks + sweetened condensed milk.
Coat widely a cake mould with caramel, and add the preparation.
To let cook with the bain-marie, in the furnace, during 45 min with 200°C (th 6-7).
Once the cooking finished, leave the dish still 30 min in the oven turned off.
Let cool well, before putting in the fridge.
Turn over only at the time of serving (be careful with the juice...).

CHESTNUT MILK CARAMEL CREAM (LACTOSE FREE)

very easy

Ingredients

1l chestnut milk
100g of sugar
6 eggs trails
1 vanilla bean

Preparation

Boil the chestnut milk with the split vanilla bean and let it infuse after scraping the inside of the bean.
To prepare the caramel, put the sugar cubes in a small saucepan with 3 tablespoons of water. Put on a high heat until the sugar syrup takes on the light brown color of the caramel. Coat the caramel in the bottom of the pan.
Beat the eggs with the sugar with a whisk.
Pour gently on this preparation the boiling milk while stirring with the whip. Transverse in the mould at the caramelized bottom.
For the cooking in the bain-marie, put this mould in a container of greater height. Fill the container with boiling water up to the level of the caramel cream.
Leave to cook for 1 hour at 150°C (gas mark 5).
Leave to cool in the open oven before removing the mould.

QUICK CARAMEL CREAM

very easy

Ingredients

1 egg
1 tablespoon of flour
1 tablespoon of cornstarch
1 l of milk

Preparation

Prepare the cream:
Mix the flour, the cornstarch, the egg then add the milk. Start to heat the preparation by stirring from time to time.
Meanwhile, prepare the caramel:
a little water with sugar. As soon as it becomes well roux, out of the fire, add a little boiling water (be careful with the splashes!). Then add the caramel to the almost hot cream. When it boils, lower the heat and heat for 3 minutes while stirring.

COOKIES CARAMEL AND M&MS

very easy

Ingredients

1 egg
45ml of oil (or 50 g of soft butter)
125g of flour
1 sachet of baking powder
40g of brown sugar
2 tablespoons of creamy caramel
1 tablespoon of nutella (optional)
80g of peanut M&M's

Preparation

Preheat your oven to 200 degrees.
Start by mixing the egg (unbeaten), flour, oil, yeast and sugar in the desired order in a bowl.
Melt your caramel into a cream (I use salidou cream) for a few seconds in the microwave.
If you don't have any caramel in a jar, you can just as well melt your hard caramel in a bain marie or in the microwave (prefer the bain marie).
Add your melted caramel to the mixture.
Then add a tablespoon of Nutella (always good but not obligatory).
Put your m&m's in a plastic bag and have a blast crushing them (but not too much anyway, unless the m&m's dust plugs you in).

Stir them into the salad bowl, keeping 9 aside.
After taking care to put baking paper on your baking sheet, shape your cookies into small balls not too thick and well spaced apart from each other (their diameter will double when baking).
Place your 9 m&m's delicately on your cookies
(without pushing them too much).
Put them in the oven for 10 minutes.
During this time, watch your little darlings double in volume and smell the good smell coming out of the oven.
The ten minutes are over, yes the cookies are still soft, it's NORMAL. Take them out of the oven and let them cool down for ten minutes before any attempt to remove the cookie, which could be fatal.
Finally, the cookies have cooled and hardened on their own like big ones.
When you feel proud that you have resisted the urge to taste them, tenderly peel off your cookies and throw yourself on them!
Love cookies.

VANILLA AND ORANGE CARAMEL DESSERT CREAM

easy

Ingredients

1 orange
15 cl of water
100 g of sugar
1 sachet of vanilla sugar
2 eggs
75 cl of milk
25 g of flour

Preparation

Cut the orange peel into strips of 3 mm wide, blanch them 3 times to remove the bitterness.
Make a syrup with 15 cl of water and 100 g of sugar then plunge the peels into it.
Drain the zests and reserve the caramel.
Make a vanilla cream: boil 75 cl of milk, 30 g of sugar, 1 sachet of vanilla sugar.
In a salad bowl mix 2 whole eggs and 25 g of flour.
Add this mixture to the boiling milk off the heat, mix well, heat until thickened.
Pour the cream and lecarameld in 6 containers.
Serve well chilled.

CHOCOLATE-CARAMEL CHEESECAKE

easy

Ingredients

1 packet of sablésbreton
400g of cottage cheese (20% fat)
1 bar of chocolate dessert caramel
3 eggs
70g of butter
50g of flour
2 tablespoons of sugar
10cl of liquid cream
1 moulds to miss with removable bottom

Preparation

In a bowl, crumble the cookies and add the melted butter.
Mix and line the bottom of the pan.
Place in the refrigerator for 1 hour.
Preheat the oven to 160°C (thermostat 5-6).
In a salad bowl, mix the cottage cheese, flour, sugar and egg yolks.
Beat the egg whites until stiff and fold
them gently into the mixture.
Then, pour on the cookie base and bake in the oven for 40 min.
Leave to cool.
Prepare the ganache:

Heat the cream in the microwave oven and pour the caramel chocolate broken into pieces. Mix.
Pour the ganache over the cake and place in the refrigerator for at least 2 hours.
Serve with custard.

MELTING CARAMEL SALTED BUTTER CHOCOLATE TART

easy

Ingredients

1 shortcrust pastry
100g of white sugar
14cl of cream
20g of butter
1 level teaspoon of salt
200g of milk chocolate
1cl of cream

Preparation

Cook the shortcrust pastry according to your recipe and the time indicated. Leave to cool.
Heat the cream in the microwave until hot (this will then prevent splashing due to temperature differences and the formation of crystals).
In a saucepan, heat the sugar over medium heat until a blond caramel is formed, stirring continuously with a wooden spoon.
Add the hot cream and mix.
Add the salt and mix.
Add the butter and mix
Cook over medium heat until a medium thick cream is obtained, stirring constantly (approx. 10 min).

Let the cream cool. Pour the cream on the shortcrust pastry cooked in white. Put in the fridge
Melt the chocolate and the cream in a water bath or in the microwave at a very low heat (open the door regularly and mix to prevent the chocolate from taking on a crystalline consistency). Spread over the tart with a brush.
Put in the fridge and keep in the fridge until tasting.

CRUNCHY APPLE PIE IN SALTED BUTTERSCOTCH CREAM CARAMEL

easy

Ingredients

1 shortcrust pastry
4 apples
110g of sugar
3 egg yolks
250ml semi-skimmed milk
2/3 teaspoon of salted caramel butter (vahiné type)
almonds, butter, sugar for the crispness

Preparation

1- Preheat the oven to 200°. Put the dough in the dish.
2- Peel the apples, cut them into large cubes and arrange them on the dough.
3- Mix the egg yolks, the 110g of sugar, the milk, the maizena and the caramel. Pour over the apples.
4- Cook 35-40min
5- Brown the almonds in a frying pan over a high heat with the butter and sugar. arrange on the tart at the last moment.

CHOCOLATE CARAMEL FRUIT TART TATIN

easy

Ingredients

1 shortcrust pastry
Fruit to cover the whole shortcrust pastry.
200g of milk chocolate
30g of butter
Caramel

Preparation

Preheat your oven to 180°C (thermostat 6).
Spread the dough on a baking sheet and cover with pieces of fruit of your choice.
Bake for about 15 minutes.
During this time, melt your chocolate with the butter.
Once the tart is out of the oven, pour the chocolate over the entire surface.
Put in the fridge until the chocolate sets.
Finally, prepare your caramel and pour it over the chocolate.
Have a good appetite!

FINE APPLE, PEAR AND VANILLA CARAMEL PIE

easy

Ingredients

1 broken dough to unroll
3 tablespoons of applesauce
3 ripe pears
3 teaspoons of vanilla extract
4 pinches of brown sugar
5 half-salted butter nuts

Preparation

Unroll your dough while keeping the baking paper and prick very little.
Spread the applesauce and cut the pears into thin strips.
Add the vanilla extract, then the sugar and finally the pieces of butter.
Bake for about 25 min (depending on the oven) the caramel will make itself.
Serve slightly warm.
Bon appétit!

DARK CHOCOLATE AND SALTED BUTTER CARAMEL TARTS

easy

Ingredients

1 shortcrust pastry (approx. 230 g)
100g of sugar
3cl of water
25g of semi-salted butter
15cl of liquid cream
120g of dark chocolate

Preparation

Cut out 30 circles of dough and prick them so that they do not swell when baked.
Line 2 mini silicone tartlet moulds with the dough and place them in the freezer for 5 minutes.
Place the tart moulds on the cold grill of the oven and bake for 5 minutes in the preheated oven at 200°C (thermostat 6-7).
Remove the tart bases from the moulds and leave to cool on a cooling rack.
Caramel: In a saucepan, mix the sugar and water and cook without stirring until golden brown. Out of the fire add the semi-salted butter while stirring without stopping (be careful with the projections), add 5 cl of liquid cream and put back to cook on a low fire for 1 min, while stirring

regularly. Remove from the heat source and leave to cool.
Ganache: heat liquid cream in the microwave for 1min30 to 750watts, add the chocolate in pieces to the cream, let stand for 2 min and mix with a soft whisk.
Garnish the tart bases with the caramel and then the ganache. Leave to cool for 1 hour at room temperature.

APPLE TART, SPECULOS AND SALTED BUTTERSCOTCH CARAMEL

easy

Ingredients

1 puff pastry ready to unroll
3 apples
10 speculoos
125g of buttered butter
Sucre cassonade

Preparation

Take the deep-fried baking tray from the oven, preheat your oven to 180°C (thermostat 6).
Unroll the puff pastry in the baking tray, leaving the baking sheet in place.
Sprinkle brown sugar generously over the tart base so that the dough is almost invisible.
With a peeler make shavings of salted butter and cover the sugar.
Peel the apples, remove the core, cut thin slices and place them 1 cm from the edge of the dough.

Sprinkle the apples again generously with brown sugar.
Coarsely crush the speculoos and sprinkle over the whole.
Cover again with shavings of salted butter
and put in the oven for 30 min.
At the end of the 30 min, spend 2 min on the
grill function to perfect the caramel.
Let cool before tasting!

APPLE PIE, CHOCOLATE AND SALTED BUTTER CARAMEL

easy

Ingredients

1 ready-to-use puff pastry
100g of chocolate (dark or milk, as you like)
4 apples according to size
100g brown sugar
50g of butter and half salt

Preparation

Unroll the dough in a pie tin.
Melt the chocolate (preferably in a bain marie) and pour it over the dough.
Cut the apples into strips and place them on the chocolate to form a rosette. Sprinkle with 20g of sugar.
Bake for 15 minutes at 180°C (gas mark 6).
5 min before the end, melt the butter with the remaining sugar. Let the caramel form and dilute if necessary with water so that the caramel is liquid enough.
Pour over the apples at the end of the first cooking time and bake for 20-25 min.

MELTING APPLE AND CARAMEL PIE

easy

Ingredients

1 ready-to-use puff pastry
8 apples and imettes
3 tablespoons of liquid honey
140g powdered sugar
100g of butter
2 tablespoons of fresh cream
1 tablespoon of calvados

Preparation

Cut the apples into quarters and then into large dice.
In a frying pan, melt 50 g of butter and
pour the diced apples into it.
While cooking, pour 1 tablespoon of honey and sprinkle
with 20 g of sugar. Mix and let cook for 10 minutes
(the apples should be very lightly stewed).
Turn out the tart dough in a mould and
prick the bottom of the tart.
Pour 2 tablespoons of honey and spread with a brush.
Pour the apple pieces and the calvados and sprinkle
again with sugar.
Put in the oven for 25 mn Th 7 (180°C).
At the exit, let it cool down.
Meanwhile, prepare the caramel.

Melt 50 g of butter in a frying pan over low heat.
Add 100 g of sugar and let the caramel form.
Off the heat, add the crème fraîche and pour this mixture over the apples (NOTE: don't worry if the caramel gets thick, just spread the mixture over the tart as much as possible. As it cooks, it will melt again).
Return to the oven for 15 min Th 7 (180°C).

PEAR AND CARAMEL PIE

easy

Ingredients

1 shortbread paste
1 large box of pear
1/2 lemon
chocolate chip
75g of sugar
125g of fresh cream
2 egg yolks
25g of cornstarch
1/8l milk (12,5 cl)
1 pinch of vanilla

Preparation

Arrange the dough in a mould and pre-bake in the oven for 15 min at 160°C (thermostat 5/6), covering the bottom with dried beans.
In the meantime, make the flan: heat the cream in a saucepan. In another pan, melt 75 g of sugar and the lemon juice by turning them with a spatula. When the caramel is brown, add small amounts of cream. Set aside.
Whip the rest of the sugar with the yolks.
Add the cornflour, then the cold milk and vanilla.
Mix this mixture with the caramel mixture. Filter and set aside.
Take the tart out of the oven. Remove the beans.

Slice the pears and place them on the tart.
Cover them with the caramel custard.
Put in the oven for 15 minutes at 160°C.
Let stand and sprinkle with chocolate shavings before serving.

CHOCOLATE AND CARAMEL TART (WITH SALTED BUTTER)

easy

Ingredients

1 shortbread paste
200g of chocolate
75g of buttered butter
150g of sugar
20cl of liquid fresh cream

Preparation

Make a caramel by melting butter and sugar. When it is brown, remove from the heat and let it cool a little (to avoid the formation of lumps). Add fresh cream to give the caramel a creamy consistency (not necessarily the whole quantity, it's up to your taste). Then add the chocolate in pieces which will melt on its own in the mixture. Homogenize well. Pour on the paste that has been previously baked in white (about 25 minutes at 180°C). Put in the fridge for at least two hours. For decoration and taste you can add dried fruits (almonds, walnuts, hazelnuts, pistachios).

CARAMEL WALNUT TART

easy

Ingredients

1 shortbread paste
200g of nuts
1 can of sweetened condensed milk (397 g)
165g of caramel
125g powdered sugar
4 eggs
50g of buttered butter

Preparation

Melt salted butter, caramels and sweetened condensed milk over low heat until a smooth dough is obtained. In a bowl, beat the eggs with the powdered sugar. Add the mixture of butter, caramels and sweetened condensed milk, then the nuts. Preheat the oven to 180°C (gas mark 6). Spread the shortbread dough in a pie tin, prick it and add the preparation. Bake at the bottom of the oven on rotating heat for 40 min.

CHOCOLATE CARAMEL WALNUT TART

easy

Ingredients

1 shortbread paste
200g powdered sugar
200g of liquid cream
150g of chopped nuts
50g of dark chocolate

Preparation

Preheat the oven to 200°C (thermostat 6-7).
Line the pan with the dough, prick the bottom and sides, place in the oven until the dough is baked, about 15 to 20 minutes.
Put the sugar in a saucepan, let it caramelize while stirring continuously.
Heat the cream at the same time.
When the sugar is pale, add the boiling cream, mix well, stir in the chopped nuts and stir.
Pour over the tart base.
When the tart is cooled, melt the chocolate and coat the tart with it.

STAR TART APPLE CINNAMON CARAMEL SALTED BUTTER

easy

Ingredients

1 shortbread paste
4 tablespoons of salted butterscotch
2 apples
1/2 teaspoon cinnamon
1 egg yolk

Preparation

Cut the apples into small pieces and cook in a saucepan with half a glass of water and then add the 1/2 teaspoon of cinnamon.
Cook over low heat for about 10 minutes.
Spread the shortbread dough.
Towards the edge of the dough, spread the salted butterscotch, go all around the dough for a width of at least 5 cm.
When the apples are ready, spread them evenly over the caramel.
With a knife, make an incision in the middle of the dough and make an X-shaped incision on top.
Take the tips and bring them back to the edges to form the star.
With a brush spread the egg yolk on the dough.
Put in the oven at 180°C (thermostat 6) for 15 min.

CHOCOLATE, CARAMEL AND MASCARPONE TART

easy

Ingredients

1 homemade shortbread paste
200g of pastry chocolate
1 tablespoon of café fort
250g of mascarpone
200g of sugar
75g of buttered butter

Preparation

Prepare the homemade shortbread dough, and bake it white. Let it cool.
Prepare the chocolate ganache, by melting the chocolate with 200 g of mascarpone and a tablespoon of strong coffee in a saucepan over very very low heat (or in a bain-marie). When the mixture is melted, add the rest of the mascarpone. Spread the ganache over the shortbread dough and let rest in a cool place (at least 30 min).
Prepare the caramel. Melt the sugar with two tablespoons of water, without stirring with a utensil. When it starts to brown, add the salted butter off the heat. Mix until a homogeneous mixture is obtained, put back on low heat if small crystals have formed to melt them. For an even

smoother caramel, add a spoonful of mascarpone. Spread the caramel on the chocolate layer and put it back in the fridge for about an hour.
Enjoy!

PIE WITH 3 APPLES, ALMONDS, CINNAMON AND CARAMEL

very easy

Ingredients

1 pomme canada
1 pomme rouge
1 pomme nashi (also called apple-pear or Japanese pear) otherwise take 2 small pears
1 vanilla shortbread paste
100g of almond slivers
50g of sugar
1 small teaspoon cinnamon powder

Preparation

I invented this recipe with the ingredients I had at home. If you don't have a vanilla shortbread dough, you can take a plain shortbread dough (ready-made or homemade) and add a few drops of vanilla concentrate or the seeds of 2 vanilla beans. Spread the dough and place it in a pie dish previously lined or covered with baking paper. Using a fork, make a few holes in it. Reserve.
Peel the 3 apples, cut them into quarters, remove the cores, and cut into slices of about 3 mm.
Mix all the apples well together.
Arrange them on the dough, sprinkle with

slivered almonds and cinnamon.
Bake at 180° (gas mark 6) for 20 minutes.
Once the cooking is finished, prepare the caramel.
Put the sugar in a saucepan (without water) on high heat and wait for the sugar to caramelize.
After a few minutes, the sugar melts and then becomes colored. Do not touch it during the cooking process.
When the liquid is well colored (light and golden color) but without turning brown, remove from the heat.
Immediately afterwards (the caramel hardens very quickly) pour into a small bowl. Using a spoon, drip filaments or drops of caramel onto the still hot tart.
If the caramel has hardened too quickly, don't panic, crush the contents of the bowl with a mortar or anything hard, solid and flat that fits in your bowl and sprinkle the caramel crystals over the pie.
Bake again for 5 minutes, watching the baking process.
Serve warm or cold.

EASY CARAMEL CAKE

very easy

Ingredients

1 jar of caramel dessert cream (use the jar as the unit of measure for the other ingredients)
2 jars of sugar
3 pots of flour
2 eggs
1 tablespoon of oil
1 sachet of yeast
15 caramelmous (approximately, can be adapted according to taste)

Preparation

Start by emptying the cream jar into a bowl, clean the jar with water and wipe it well.
In a bowl, mix the flour, sugar and yeast.
Add the eggs, the caramel cream and the oil.
Cut the sweets into 3 or 4 pieces and add them to the dough.
Mix well to distribute them well in the preparation.
Pour in a previously oiled mould and put in the oven for about 45 minutes at thermostat 5/6 (165°C).

VERRINE MASCARPONE PEAR CARAMEL

very easy

Ingredients

1 pot of mascarpone
2 eggs
62g of sugar
1 sachet of vanilla sugar
1 large box of leeks in syrup
1 box of Breton palets
1 pinch of salt
Caramel liquid

Preparation

Separate the whites from the yolks.
Beat the whites with a pinch of salt until they are very firm.
Add the sugar and beat until you obtain a shiny meringue.
Pour the mascarpone, vanilla sugar and egg yolks
into a bowl and beat with a whisk.
Add the meringue to this bowl and mix well.
Crumble the palets. Cut the pears in small pieces.
Fill the verrines in the following way: mascarpone - cookie - fruit - caramel and repeat the same up to the top of the verrine.

CHOCOLATE CHIP MUFFINS WITH SALTED BUTTER CARAMEL HEART

very easy

Ingredients

1 jar of stirred yogurt
2 jars of flour
1/2 jar of oil
2 eggs
1 jar of sugar
1 sachet of baking powder
50g of chocolate

Preparation

We start with caramel :
Put the sugar in the microwave for 3 min without stirring until it turns into an amber liquid (you have to be careful).
During this time, heat the liquid cream
so that it is just simmering.
As soon as the sugar has turned into an amber liquid, add the lukewarm liquid cream, paying attention to the splashes.
Stir, quickly add the butter, and stir again,
until the sauce is creamy.

Put the mixture back into the microwave, stirring every 30 s, for 2 to 3 min, which will allow any pieces of caramel to melt. Add the salt and stir again. Pour the sauce into a glass jar, cover and set aside at room temperature.
Separate the yolk from the whites. Whisk the whites until stiff and set aside.
Mix the egg yolks and sugar, then add the oil. Add the stirred yoghurt.
Stir in the flour and baking powder, then the chocolate chips (or nuggets), at the end add the egg whites, mix gently with a spatula. Put a little dough in the moulds, and on top a tablespoon of caramel. Cover with another layer of pastry.
Bake for 25 min at 180° (thermostat 6).

APPLE, SPICE AND CARAMEL CAKE

very easy

Ingredients

1 pot of yoghurt of fresh cream (about 125 ml)
2 jars of sugar yoghurt
3 pots of flour
1 packet of yeast
1 packet of vanilla sugar
10cl of milk
Cinnamon
Clove
Ginger
Cumin
Pepper
star of badian
Cardamom
6 apples
100g of walnut kernel
100g of sugar
Water
2 Butter nuts

Preparation

Start by preparing the caramel. Put 100 g of sugar in a saucepan, cover it with water and bring to the boil. Then lower the heat and watch carefully: the caramel

can burn very quickly.
When the caramel starts to brown, add the butter and two tablespoons of milk - be careful to the explosion! - and mix quickly to avoid overflow.
Let cook one more minute without stopping stirring, then pour the caramel on a sheet of baking paper.
Spread to obtain a layer of about 3mm then let cool.
In the meantime, mix the yoghurt, sugars and eggs in a salad bowl. Beat vigorously, then add the flour, baking powder and spices. Mix again, add the milk, the crushed walnuts and the apples in large pieces.
The caramel has hardened: break it into pieces (about the size of a fingernail of an inch).
Add them to the dough, reserving a few for decoration.
Pour the dough into a buttered and floured mould, place the remaining pieces of caramel on top and bake for one hour at 180°C (gas mark 6).
Serve cold or warm.

EASY CHOCOLATE AND CARAMEL MOUSSE

easy

Ingredients

1 bar of chocolate
4 eggs
5 tablespoons of sugar

Preparation

Do not unpack the chocolate bar yet and hit it against a table to break it.
Unwrap the bar and finish breaking it with your hands.
Pour in the chocolate pieces, then set the cooking temperature to low and help the cooking by stirring a little.
While the chocolate is melting, break the eggs, separating the white from the yolk.
Pour the yolks into the saucepan where the chocolate melts and stir to mix well.
Pour the whites into a bowl and beat them until stiff.
Put the sugar in a bowl then after mixing it with water, pour into a saucepan and cook over low heat.
When the whites are well beaten, pour the pan containing the chocolate mixed with the yolks and mix well until the mixture is smooth.
When the mixture is smooth and the sugar has

turned into caramel, distribute the mousse in the bowls and cover them with the caramel.
Put in the fridge, wait a few hours and serve!

CHOCO-CARAMEL MUFFINS, SALTED BUTTER

easy

Ingredients

1 bar of caramel chocolate
70g of flour
80g of sugar
100g of buttered butter
2 eggs
2 tablespoons of fresh cream

Preparation

Melt 130 g of choco-caramel with the butter cut into small cubes. Add the flour, sugar and eggs. (For more airy muffins, beat the egg whites until stiff and fold in).
Add the fresh cream.
Cut the remaining chocolate into small pieces (in the form of chips) and add them to the mixture.
Divide into muffin cups.
Bake at 210° (th. 7) 12 min, and enjoy!

CHEESE, APPLE AND CARAMEL CAKE

very easy

Ingredients

1 cup of flour
1/2 cup margarine or butter
3/4 cup of sugar
1 egg yolk
2 tablespoons of margarine
2 apples, peeled, cored and thinly sliced
Caramel liquid
1 teaspoon of milk
500g of cream cheese (type St moret, Gervais frais...)
1 teaspoon of vanilla
2 eggs
Toasted hazelnuts, chopped

Preparation

CROUTE:
Mix well together flour, 1/2 cup margarine, 1/4 cup sugar and egg yolk. Press at the bottom and on 1 (2.5 cm) from the edges of a 9" hinged mold. (23 cm). Bake in the oven at 200°C, 15 mn.
FILLING:
Melt 2 tablespoons of margarine in a large frying pan. Add apples; cook until tender. Arrange on crust. Mix liquid caramel and milk, stirring over

low heat; pour over apples.

In large mixer bowl, beat cream cheese, 1/2 cup sugar and vanilla. Add eggs, one at a time. Pour over caramel layer.

Bake at 160°C for 35 minutes or until cake is firm.

Let cool; refrigerate. Slice and serve with the caramel sauce and hazelnuts. Makes 12 servings.

Caramel sauce (optional):

Melt 1/2 cup liquid caramel and 1/4 cup milk, stirring over low heat.

YOGHURT AND CARAMEL SALTED BUTTERSCOTCH CAKE

easy

Ingredients

1 natural yogurt (pot to be reused to measure the other ingredients)
2 jars of flour
2 jars of sugar
1/2 jar of oil
1/2 bag of yeast
3 eggs

Preparation

In a salad bowl, pour the yoghurt, sugar and mix. Add the flour, the eggs and then the yeast. Finish with the oil.
Mix everything together to obtain a homogeneous paste.
Butter then flour your mould and pour the preparation into it.
Preheat your oven to 180°C (thermostat 6), in the meantime, we will prepare our caramel.
Heat the sugar in a saucepan over medium heat without stirring. You may want to rotate the pan to distribute the sugar evenly during cooking.
You should obtain a smooth sugar that is nicely colored.
Heat your cream and add it to the sugar, off the heat. If the cream is poured cold or at room temperature, you will get lumps

in your caramel, which is not the purpose of this recipe. Incorporate the salted butter (or butter + pinch of salt) and put back on the fire while mixing a few moments. Gently pour the caramel over the dough (not all at once, otherwise all the caramel would fall to the bottom), but in small touches here and there.
Bake the cake for about 15 minutes at 180°C (thermostat 6) according to the oven, knowing that the cake must be colored and the tip of your knife must come out dry.
Bon appétit!

PEAR-CARAMEL YOGHURT CAKE

easy

Ingredients

1 yogurt (about 125g)
1 jar of powdered sugar + 2 tablespoons
2 egg trails
2 jars of flour
2 teaspoons of baking yeast
1 half jar of sunflower oil
2 pears
Water

Preparation

Put the yoghurt in a bowl.
Keep the jar for the following quantities:
Add 1 jar of sugar and the eggs
Mix.
Add 2 jars of flour and baking powder.
Mix.
Add 1/2 jar of oil.
Mix.
Add the pears cut into pieces.
Preparation of the caramel:
Put a bottom of water in a small saucepan.
Put 2 tablespoons of sugar in it.
Make heat until obtaining a clear caramel.

Add to the preparation.
Preheat your oven to 180°C.
Put in the oven for about 35 minutes.

CARAMEL WITH SALTED BUTTER INRATABLE

easy

Ingredients

200g of butter salé cut in dices,
1 briquette of liquid crème fraîche entière,
400g caster sugar,
4 tablespoons of liquid honey.

Preparation

Put sugar and honey in a saucepan over medium heat.
Mix until you obtain a mahogany-colored caramel
(according to your taste).
Pour the whole HOT fresh cream with caramel (be careful with
the projections but if your cream is hot, there is no problem).
Boil for 3 minutes while mixing well, there
should be no more lumps of caramel.
Remove from the heat and add the salted butter in dices
and mix well, the butter must melt completely.
Put in a pot and voilà!

BANANA CHEESECAKE WITH CARAMEL SAUCE

Average level

Ingredients

200g of biscuit genre
Sprits
80g of melted butter
4 ripe bananas
4 eggs
6 Swiss children
450g of cheese type St Morêt
150g powdered sugar
1 tablespoon cinnamon powder
1 lemon juice extract
300g of caramel
2 yaourts brewed type Velvety

Preparation

These proportions are given for a springform pan
or a pastry circle of 24 cm diameter.
Preheat the oven to 180°C (gas mark 6).
Put the cookies in a freezer bag and crush them with a rolling pin.
When they are in crumbs, mix them with the melted butter.
Press this mixture well into the bottom of the tin
and put them in the oven for 10 minutes.
Take the pan out of the oven and lower the temperature
to 140°C (thermostat 4-5).

Prepare the cream: mash the bananas with a
fork and sprinkle with lemon juice.
Add the fromage frais and the petits-suisses and mix with an
electric whisk (minimum speed) for about 30 seconds.
Then add the sugar, then the eggs, one by one, and
finally the cinnamon, beating the mixture only as
long as it takes to incorporate the ingredients.
Pour the cream on the bottom of the dough and
put in the oven for 1 hour of cooking.
To prevent cracks from forming on the cheesecake,
cooling is a crucial step!
The cheesecake does not tolerate sudden temperature changes.
Once the cheesecake is cooked, switch off the oven and leave it
in the oven with the door closed for 1-2 hours, then take it out
and wait until it has cooled completely before removing it from
the mould and putting it in the refrigerator for at least 24 hours.
Prepare the sauce just before serving:
Unwrap the caramels in a saucepan and
melt them over very low heat.
Add the yoghurts and mix well, always over low
heat, until a homogeneous sauce is obtained.
Just before serving, decorate the cheesecake with
bananas cut into thin slices, sprinkle with a few drops
of lemon juice and sprinkle with cinnamon.

SPARKLING CARAMBAR BAVARIAN OR CARAMEL BAVAROIS

easy

Ingredients

200g of carambar© (= 24 carambars)
1.5 gelatin sheets
200g of fresh cream liquidENTIERE (not lightened!)
60g of milk

Preparation

About 30 minutes before starting the recipe, put the liquid cream in the freezer, the whips of the mixer and a high rimmed salad bowl in the refrigerator.
Peel the carambars.
Soften the gelatine leaf in cold water.
In a small saucepan, heat the milk with the carambars over low heat while stirring continuously. You should obtain a kind of creamy caramel sauce. Add the well-drained gelatine and stir carefully. Let it cool down but not too much otherwise the mixture will harden.
Pour your cold cream into the bowl. Then gently beat the cream with the electric whisks.

At the beginning you put them on low power because otherwise you will line your kitchen. It would be a pity! When the cream starts to thicken, you can increase the power of the mixer. We stop whipping when the cream has thickened and sticks to the branches of the whip. Be careful not to beat too long, otherwise you will get butter. You can help you in this operation with a sachet of whipped cream fixative (available in all supermarkets).
Gently fold your whipped cream into your carambar cream. Line 4 ramekins (or 6 if you are reasonable gourmets!) with stretch film (make sure the film is larger than the size of the ramekin. The excess will be used to cover the ramekins). Distribute the preparation in each ramekin. Cover with the stretch film and put it in the fridge for at least 2 hours.
At serving time, unmould, remove the plastic film. Decorate with a little cocoa powder.

CHOCOLATE MOUSSE AND SALTED BUTTER CARAMEL

Average level

Ingredients

200g of milk chocolate
3 eggs
100g of sugar
40g of buttered butter
20cl of liquid cream

Preparation

Prepare the caramel by heating the sugar and 2 tablespoons of water. As soon as the mixture blondizes, add the butter, then remove from the heat and pour in the cream. Put back on the heat while stirring to obtain a smooth caramel. Remove from the heat, add the chocolate in pieces and stir until melted. Let cool and then add the egg yolks. Let cool well before incorporating the egg whites whisked in snow. To put in small pots or ramekins. Then place in the refrigerator at least 6 hours.

CHOCOLATE/ CARAMEL MELTING HEART HALF-COOKED

easy

Ingredients

200g of dark chocolate
100g of butter
70g of flour
180g of cane sugar
5 eggs
1 tablespoon of skimmed milk
Caramel with salemou butter

Preparation

Preheat the oven to 200°C.
Melt the chocolate and butter in a saucepan over low heat.
Add the milk.
At the same time, mix the eggs and sugar.
Pour the melted chocolate into the sweet mixture.
Sprinkle the flour.
Put in the oven moulds.
Leave to bake for about 4 min (out of the 10 min necessary for the baking of the mi-cuit), before digging a small hole to pour the caramel (jam or spread), otherwise insert a piece of soft caramel in the middle of the mi-cuit before putting it in the oven.

MELTING BROWNIES WITH CARAMEL TASTE

very easy

Ingredients

200g of dark chocolate
1 box of milk jam (recipe on the site)
150g of fresh cheese (kiri type)
2 eggs + 2 yolks
Vanilleliquide
50g brown sugar
50g of butter
Nuts

Preparation

Mix the eggs, sugar and 2 teaspoons of vanilla with an electric mixer until the mass whitens and doubles in volume. Melt the chocolate with the butter until the mixture is smooth. Add to the eggs the chocolate mixture, the milk jam and the fresh cheese. Add the nuts and mix well. Bake in a hot oven for about 30 minutes.
(To complete this dessert I make a caramel to which I add a little butter and cream. Once the brownies have cooled, I cover them with the caramel and sprinkle them with praline).

EASY CHOCOLATE AND CARAMEL CHEESECAKE

easy

Ingredients

200g of dark chocolate
40cl of fresh cream
2 packets of chocolate-filled cookies
150g of butter
1 can of sweetened condensed milk
1 teaspoon of powdered gelatin

Preparation

Grind the cookies in a blender. Gradually add the melted butter until a dry dough is obtained. Spread evenly on the bottom of a springform pan with the back of a spoon. Set aside in the freezer.
In a pressure cooker, put the closed milk can, cover it with water and cook over low heat to make caramel.
Beat half of the fresh cream into whipped cream.
Warm up the rest of the cream. Off the heat,
add the dark chocolate. Stir to melt.
Add half of the gelatine previously warmed in the microwave with a teaspoon of water.
Once the condensed milk has become caramel, add the whipped cream and the other half of the gelatine.
Spread the caramel mixture over the cookie. Let stand in the

freezer for 15 minutes before adding the chocolate mixture.

IMPRINT

All rights reserved

Mindful Publishing
We help you to publish your book!
By

TTENTION Inc.
Wilmington - DE19806
Trolley Square 20c

All rights reserved

Instagram: mindful_publishing
Contact: mindful.publishing@web.de
Contact2: mindful.publishing@protonmail.com

Made in United States
Troutdale, OR
01/03/2024

16677830R00046